SYDNEY'S ADVENTURES
SLIDING INTO SUMMER

**WRITTEN BY
STEPHANIE DIEHL**

**STORYBOARDS BY
NOAM LEVI**

**PAINTING BY
TRULY SANDRA**

Sydney's Adventures
Copyright © 2024 by Stephanie Diehl

All rights reserved. No part of this publication may be reproduced, distributed, or transmitted in any form or by any means, including photocopying, recording, or other electronic or mechanical methods, without the prior written permission of the author, except in the case of brief quotations embodied in critical reviews and certain other noncommercial uses permitted by copyright law.

For permissions requests, contact author at info@stephaniediehl.com or www.stephaniediehl.com

Library of Congress Cataloging-in-Publication data is available
ISBN: (Hardback) 979-8-218-35334-6

First edition 2024

Stephanie Diehl
Middletown, CA

www.stephaniediehl.com

"BUT THE FRUIT OF THE SPIRIT IS
LOVE, JOY, PEACE, PATIENCE,
KINDNESS, GOODNESS, FAITHFULNESS,
GENTLENESS, SELF-CONTROL; AGAINST SUCH THINGS THERE IS NO LAW."
GALATIANS 5:22-23

Today is the start of Sydney's summer vacation! Every year her family takes an **EXTRAVAGANT TRiP** after school lets out.

This year, the family chose between a cruise and a safari expedition.

Sydney had her heart set on the safari, but the final choice was left up to a coin. Coin flips are something fun her family does when they want an **EXCiTiNG WAY TO CHOOSE AN ADVENTURE**. But Sydney realized that it's not always so exciting when the coin doesn't land your way.

When it was time for her family to board the ship, Sydney was still upset about the safari.

She **WiSHED** there were boots and a hat inside of her suitcase instead of a bathing suit and flip flops.

Sydney's mom could see the disappointment in her face, so she stopped and **WiNKED** at her.

"I know you're upset about the coin flip, but maybe you should try seeing this experience from a **DiFFERENT PERSPECTiVE**.

There is **ALWAYS AN ADVENTURE** waiting for you if you open your heart to it."

Sydney tried to pick out **SOMETHiNG GOOD** around her and noticed her baby brother clapping excitedly.

Smiling, she thought to herself that maybe there was an **ADVENTURE BREWiNG**. The massive cruise ship certainly was grand. Huge staircases lead seven stories up, windows lined the walls from corner to corner, sunshine spilled in from all directions and there were so many people! The sights and sounds gave her **HOPE** for the week ahead.

Maybe this ship did hold some hidden possibilities!

Then, as they walked onto the top deck towards their room, Sydney saw it. The **BiGGEST WATER SLiDE** she had ever laid her eyes on! It was taller than the entire ship and brighter than the sun with seemingly impossible twists and turns. At the end, the slide reached out over the ocean and at another it tunneled inside the ship.

SYDNEY SHUDDERED. There was no way she was ever going to get on that thing! Fear set in as she considered how much she hated the feeling of dark tunnels, cold water and stinging eyes.

The next day, Sydney got to go to **KiD'S CLUB!** She was thrilled about the arcade games, mini golf, movie theater and snacks!

After half a day of happily playing, Sydney was just about to go back to the ice cream station when she saw a new girl with big red buns and a worried face check into the club.

As Sydney added extra sprinkles to her sundae, she saw the girl walk over to the corner of the room and sit down all by herself with tears in her eyes.

Thinking the girl must be scared, and **WANTiNG TO EASE HER FEARS**, Sydney walked over to the girl and asked if she could sit down. The girl looked away from Sydney with a silent eye roll.

Sydney really wanted to be **KiND** anyway, so she asked about the girl's name. But the girl didn't even blink. She simply stood up and walked away.

WHOA, that wasn't very kind at all, thought Sydney. And for the rest of the day she moped around the games, reluctant to have any fun after her **SOUR ENCOUNTER.**

At the end of the day, Sydney's mom picked her up from Kid's Club, knowing something was wrong by the look on Sydney's face.

While tears poured down her face, Sydney told her Mom all about the girl and how she'd tried to be nice and was treated so rudely in return.
"I'm never going back there again," grouched Sydney. "She ruined Kid's Club for me!"

After she listened to the story, Sydney's mom encouraged her to "**REMEMBER THE FRUiT**."

"Even when people show us their worst, it's our job to see the good in them. When we see the good in people no matter what, our lives will always be richer with **LOVE AND CONNECTiON**.

That girl was probably scared and shy. You never know who the person underneath those hard feelings is until you give her another chance by choosing to **SEE THE GOOD** in her."

Sydney's mom always knew how to cheer her up. From that moment, she chose, yet again, to see the good and practice showing love even if the girl didn't show it back.

The next day at Kid's Club, as Sydney headed to the mini golf greens, she heard the announcement that she was dreading:

iT WAS WATER SLiDE DAY!

All the kids were going to be paired up with a partner for the day. Partners would wait in the line AND go down the slide together.

As Sydney considered her fear of the slide, a crew member walked over to introduce her partner for the day. And much to her dismay, she was standing face to face with the red headed girl once again.

Her name was Harper and she didn't even make eye contact as Sydney managed half a smile to say hello.

As they stood in line silently, Sydney remembered what her mother said the night before. Would it be worth it to try to see some good in this rude girl? Where would she even start?

Wanting to do her best to always **REMEMBER THE FRUiT**, Sydney tried once more. "I have been dreading this thing since the moment I saw it. How high does a water slide really need to be?! This is too much. I'd rather be on the mini golf greens. What about you?"

And then to Sydney's delight and surprise, Harper answered her! "Really?! You're scared of the water slide too? You seemed so **CONFiDENT AND BRAVE** when you said hi to me before. I would have never thought you were scared of anything."

As they chatted, Sydney learned that Harper was terrified during her first day at Kid's Club.

She was so scared, she couldn't bring herself to speak which is why she had acted the way she did. Sydney understood and Harper **APOLOGiZED** for being rude.

Then, the girls played a game of "This or That" to get to know each other while they climbed the spiral staircase.

As they neared the top, they discussed their fears and **WHAT iT MEANS TO BE BRAVE.**

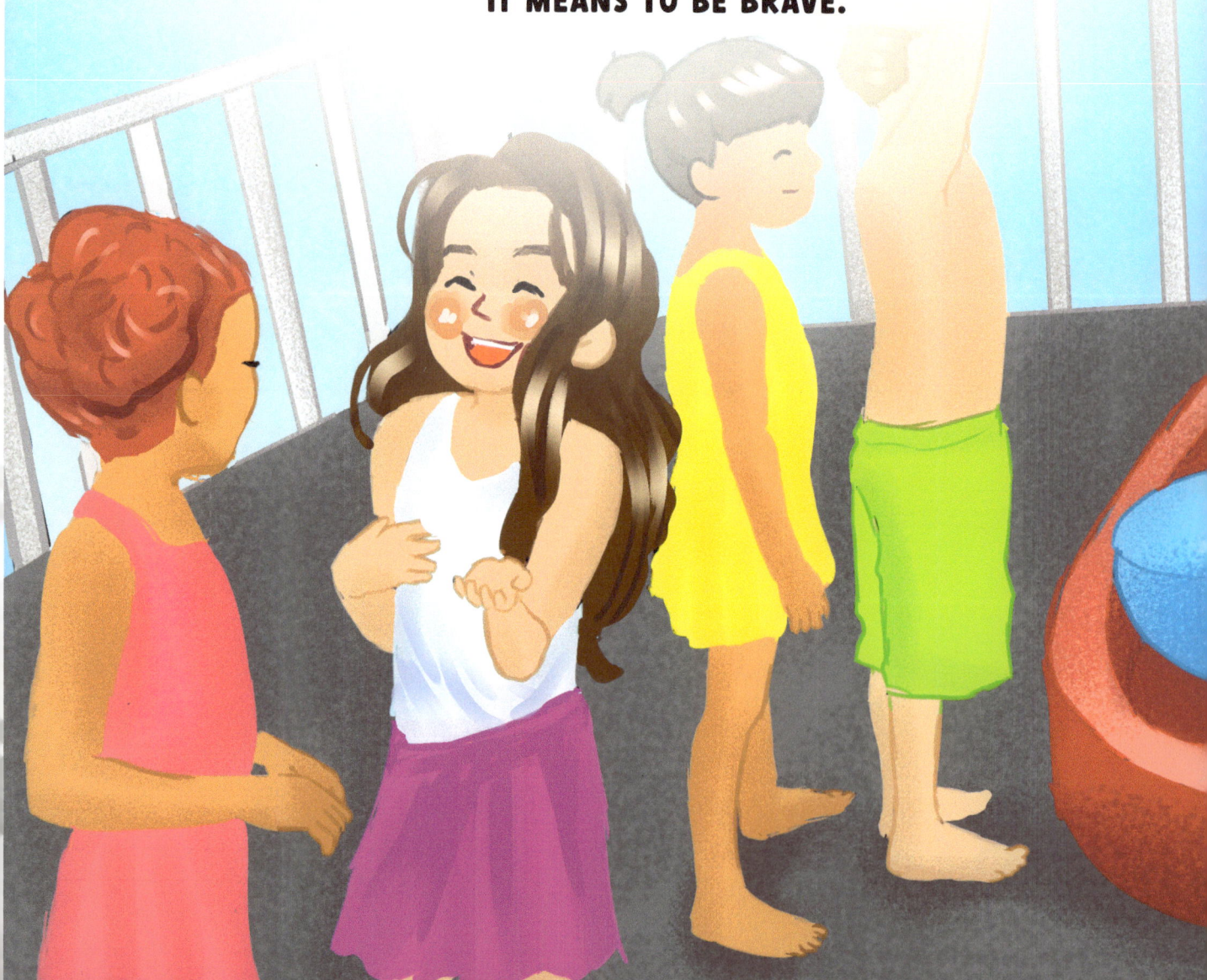

"Being brave doesn't mean not being afraid. Being brave means doing something even though you are scared," said Sydney.

"I never thought of it that way!" exclaimed Harper. "I guess it is okay to be scared as long as you **FACE THOSE FEARS** along the way."

Sydney also taught Harper what her mother told her about remembering the fruit and how important it is to always try and see the good in people and situations. "We love others by choosing to **SEE THE BEST** in them, even when they show us their worst."

They were so deep in conversation that, before they knew it, it was their turn to face their fears!

When their tube was handed to them, Sydney was not quite ready to climb in. Harper waited patiently and told her to take her time.

Once Sydney felt safe, she took a couple **DEEP BREATHS** and climbed in, making sure to hold the handles extra tight.

At first, Sydney had her eyes closed and her head down.

But when she heard Harper **LAUGH** behind her, she opened her eyes in amazement! The inside of the tunnel was a spectacle of lights and the water was warm as it splashed them at the **LOOPS AND TURNS.**

The girls even saw a whale when the slide went out over the ocean!

When they reached the end of their long and **THRILLING RIDE**, they were both sad that the **ADVENTURE WAS OVER.**

"Wow," Sydney said.
"Incredible," Harper replied.

The girls hugged and promised that next time they wouldn't allow fear or the negative feelings of others to cloud their experience.

They both agreed that **SHOWiNG KiNDNESS** (even when you don't receive it in return) is always the best option.

And that choosing to see the best of situations and people is the bravest way to have an adventure!

Sydney was so thankful her mom reminded her to **REMEMBER THE FRUiT**.

Otherwise she wouldn't have met such an awesome friend!

At the end of the week, Sydney and Harper pinky promised to stay in touch.

They knew their **ADVENTURES** bonded them for life, and they couldn't wait to get home and tell the rest of their friends all about it!

DEDICATION

This book is dedicated to Lilly. A beautiful girl, inside and out. A loving daughter, sister, and friend. A girl that was a bright light to all that were blessed to know her. Lilly, you had a huge impact on my life and my faith. I didn't know you as well as others did, but that impact says wonders of your character and spirit. Your smile is one I will always hold dear to my heart and the love, kindness, and joy you gave to all, is something that will never be forgotten. A huge thank you to Lilly's parents for allowing me to dedicate this book to their sweet angel.

#LOVEFORLILLY

MEET THE AUTHOR

Stephanie Diehl is a biological and adoptive mom of two, wife of 13 years, business owner, and blogger. She and her family enjoy living on a quiet 3 acres in the California country, where she and her husband own and manage real estate investments.

After writing for a mom blog in Sonoma County, she ventured into writing a blog of her own, where she features inspirational lifestyle content.

Faith is central to Stephanie's life, which is why she spends her time encouraging mamas and business owners to live out their God-given gifts no matter what season of life they find themselves in.

She hopes that, with this children's book series, moms and their kids are inspired to live bravely by discovering that adventure is always around them.

To keep up with the Sydney's Adventures book series, follow Stephanie on social media:

Instagram: @stephaniediehl_
Website: www.stephaniediehl.com
Email: info@stephaniediehl.com

There are Sydney's Adventures freebies and print-outs on her website.

You can also write a letter to Sydney!
Mail it here:
PO Box 129
Middletown, CA, 95461

NOW GO OUT THERE + BE BRAVE

Milton Keynes UK
Ingram Content Group UK Ltd.
UKHW050237290324
440348UK00002B/17